Picture Walking Pe(

Trevi, Spoleto, Assisi, Lake `
Montefalco, Bevagna , Spello

© Vivien Uff 05/05/2018

Think of Italy in winter on icy cold days with vicious winds gusting round every corner but with blue skies overlooking clear views in every direction: perfect walking holiday conditions for well-wrapped bodies without any crowds – anywhere! Landlocked Umbria, rolling terrain of grassy woodland and farms dotted with walled, medieval picture-perfect hill top villages on ancient volcanic plugs bounded by the snow capped high Apennines 'backbone of Italy' to the east: flowing Sagrantino wine, great coffee everywhere, tasty food, wonderful service, luxurious palace accommodation and a tiny minibus for daily trips = ideal for the *Uffs!*

This 'book' includes over 140 photos of what we saw in 7 days with a ***Ramblers' Adagio*** group holiday in March 2018. Further details of famous artists, churches and notorious characters leading inter-city rivalries before the Unification of Italy are left to the experts. The 2015 (9[th)]) edition of 'The Rough Guide to Tuscany and Umbria' includes a Directory of Artists and Architects and concise historical contexts section.

1   *Trevi* is stunning on top of its commanding site.

East of the Tiber in a parallel valley, perched high above the Vale of Spoleto, relatively unvisited Trevi was our base in the heart of Italy's finest olive groves. It's an ideal sight-seeing and easy contour walking base within a short drive of many picturesque towns. Restricted by daily visits elsewhere and 6pm sunsets we didn't see all its treasures but it's an ideal location *'far from the madding crowd'* (Hardy) in hot sunshine. Most of the shops and cafes, apart from newsagents, fresh produce and hairdressers, were due to reopen a week later for Easter and tourists.

It is literally full of former palaces and churches with two museums, a sports' centre and theatre, surrounded by olive groves and many walking trails. There's a 39 point walkabout on Trevi's free town tear-off map, masses to see and do.

Its beautiful setting epitomises the story behind many easily defended Italian hill towns, rich families keeping safe inside old Roman walls.

It's easy to visit by car or tourist bus but the train station is 4km downhill involving taxis for non-walkers. Hotels readily send transport on request. Some mobile homes were parked beside the Sports' centre outside the city walls ready to be joined by many others in warmer weather. The old town could never be overcrowded as traffic is restricted and no minibuses are permitted past the tower below.

We walked across the Ç13 Piazza Mazzini with its Civic Tower and Palazzo Comunale (Town Hall) from our usual mini bus stop in spacious Piazza Garibaldi to climb up steep cobbled alleyways to our delightful Ç16 Antica Dimora alla Rocca palace hotel almost on top of the original Ç1 double walled Roman town. A second palace opposite has extra bedrooms and an outdoor pool just across from the public restaurant entrance, a lift or short walk downhill away for us.

Our knees were glad they didn't live in the steep-sided non-vehicular streets but Italians built these narrow canyons to prevent direct sunshine in summer temperatures of 40°.

Note the arches supporting neighbouring buildings, holding hands across narrow streets, as explained in my earlier KDP.amazon.com/ *Picture Walking Around Viterbo*. Shallow foundations on hard base rock and ever-present earthquake threats necessitate these throughout these hill-top settlements.

Forecasted as 6°C most days but feeling much less: hats, scarves, gloves and anoraks were essential with rucksacks to off-load into when able to shelter from the wind or when it decided to let sunshine dominate.

Olives surrounded us along the dry, easy contour paths surrounding medieval Trevi, especially along a former aqueduct in this famous virgin oil production area.

Roberto, our hotel manager, demonstrated differences in quality between sunflower, mixed source blends and his farm's local single-origin first pressing. It's thicker, darker, more flavoursome and probably double the price of the others in supermarkets in the UK. His Mama refuses to use anything else for home cooking despite some modern chefs' theories that it can disguise subtle flavours of certain ingredients like fish. She simply uses less of the best quality oil where just a touch is needed.

Our 4 course hotel dinners were taken in its acclaimed restaurant, generous and flavoursome, breakfasts likewise. Wine, still and sparkling water were free! Totally unlimited for a nightly party atmosphere!

Spring flowers were heralding warmer weather on the roadsides ready for colourful displays later. Olive stems pruned from larger branches were simply left between trees (see below) to be trodden underfoot for future humus.

Palm Sunday ceremonies involve leaving olive sprays outside front doors after being carried there in church processions though the town. (See the photos and descriptions in the Trasimeno and Spello sections).

A lone farmer with a small ladder on his van was seen gathering the last of the black olives while on his pruning rounds.

Roberto told us nets are placed around a tree while the branches are shaken vigorously (sometimes by a mobile machine) to let the fruit fall to the ground when harvesting in autumn. It is clearly not labour intensive but demands a lot of single use farmland like the orchards spotted nearby.

The harshest winter for many years had frozen whole trees round Christmas leaving blackened leaves and anxiety about 2018's harvest. The trees seemed to have recovered as they stood in their regiments along the hillsides, ready to blossom like the wayside flowers. Truffles are a rare side benefit from olive and fruit trees, sometimes found near the roots, grated into many expensive dishes. They are hugely expensive but a little goes a long way to give a distinctive flavour in pasta, soup, omelettes etc. Our restaurant was known for them.

The snow capped hills of the Apennines in the east reminded us that Italy's ski season was enjoying perfect conditions in the Dolomites to the north. The snowline shrank gradually higher during our week, noticeably clinging to north facing slopes, a lovely sight under blue skies and powder-puff cumulus (set-fair) clouds. Olive groves, farms, hamlets and cypress tree filled the Vale of Spoleto below.

Isolated industrial sites crop up beside the railway and main roads without spoiling the open countryside at all. Factories spotted included olive processing, building materials and (Pyramid) sports' wear with the usual car, kitchen, furniture and home improvement showrooms. Like rural English villagers, Trevi residents have to drive out-of-town for these.

In my Cornish village (kdp.amazon.com/vivien uff/Picture Walking St Mawes) you have to catch a ferry to Falmouth opposite or use a bus or car to reach Truro to buy anything more than everyday groceries. They don't even have mains gas. Electricity didn't arrive until 1948, maybe not here either.

Trevi developed where 3 main routes met. Remnants of the ancient Via Flaminia (seen at various points during our travels) connected it to Ancona in the Adriatic and major cities in the north. Cooling springs set between willow trees just southwest of Trevi were frequented by Roman emperors Caligula and Claudius and poets like Byron on the 'Grand Tour' who declared the Fonti del Clitunno 'the sweetest wave of the most living crystal...the purest god of gentle waters' (p.468, Rough Guide). How *Romantic* and exaggerated!

We just caught the caretaker before closing time to let us walk around the UNESCO Tempietta del Clitunno with an exposed section of the Via Flaminia below it.

It looks truly Roman but is an Ç8 Christian church built with columns taken from collapsed temples and villas. The Byzantine frescoes of Christ, St Peter and St Paul in the alcove reminded us of many seen in Albania on a pioneer Rambler's walking holiday a few years previously.

Most of our group didn't manage to explore Trevi's museum or walk round the *Trevi Footsteps* 39 point trail but saw the exhibition which included some Roman pieces and Ç15 ceiling frescoes in the Villa Fabri just off Piazza Garibaldi. It's free and has spectacular views in all directions from its outside terraces. Trevi's Ç1st Roman city walls drop away steeply here by the Porto del Lago.

Trevi's theatre often gives young opera singers and musicians opportunities to perform but, sadly, not in our week. However we were treated to some church music one day from a young performer playing the organ. His belongings were on his bicycle outside the church, everything he needed on his 'pilgrimage' from church to church.

Italians love all forms of art and encourage young talents. Inexpensive off-peak theatre hire and free use of organs are examples (see notice over page).

2 *Spoleto*

With Bronze Age origins the colony of Spoletium developed round a crag in a very commanding position in 241 BC. It resisted Hannibal in 217BC after he had conquered Trasimeno leading him to go south to capture Rome. In the age of the *Grand Tour* Ç19 poets like Percy Bysshe Shelley described it as 'the most romantic city I ever saw' (*Rough Guide to Tuscany and Umbria,* p 472).

Its free **outside escalator** to the summit of the old town and further underground **travelator/lift** system were, happy reminders of cool journeys to work in Hong Kong and getting about Monaco. Summer heat would make the climb between upper and lower Spoleto too arduous for this tourist *honeypot*.

The internationally acclaimed June/July annual Festival dei due Monde, begun by composer Carlo Menotti in 1958, brought EU funding for this marvellous tourist facility.

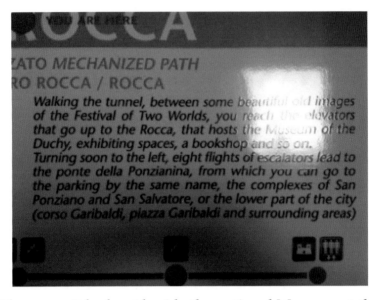

The summit lookout beside the national Museum at the Rocca d'Albornoziana fortress shows the city layout below (smudged by the telephoto lens) with its 2 Roman amphitheatres and crumbling walls. The 2nd view shows the lower town which was bombed by the Allies in WWII.

The Ponte Delle Torri (bridge of towers) Roman aqueduct is just a short walk along the Via del Ponte. It stretches 240 m over the Tessini gorge but visitors can't walk over the bridge path nowadays because of its delicate state.

Views are wonderful with some convenient cafes taking advantage but not overcharging. It's very noticeable how willing, attentive and efficient Italian waiters are. They rarely write coffee orders down but manage to get the variations right. The coffee is good if you remember to add a description of how you like it. *Caffe* is the tiniest espresso. *Americano* gives a longer black unless milk (latte) is specified, hot or cold (caldo or freddo) and exactly how hot you want it (molto, molto, molto) very, very, very hot.

Steps lead down to the spectacular 1198 cathedral of Sant'
Maria Assunta in the Piazza del Duomo, the 2nd stop on the
wondrous free escalator. Consecrated after being rebuilt
where Barbarossa had previously flattened a Ç VII church. It
has Romanesque and Renaissance delights with a
complicated history of aspects of its development and
building styles.

The *Rough Guide* describes how In 1467 Lorenzo de' Medici lent his famous Florentine painter, Filippo Lippi, to paint the frescoes of the virgin's life. Lippi was apparently poisened soon after finishing these for seducing a Spoletan nobleman's daughter, his philandering being the reason Medici had wanted him out of Florence in the first place. Stories of city-state rivalry, warring factions, one-upmanship in the art stakes, poisening and general bad behaviour dominate the background history of all these wonderful buildings. Filippino, his son, designed Lippi's tomb.

The Rough Guide's Umbrian history section and its directory of artists and architects pp 547-562 plus their book recommendations are strongly recommended to fill in some of the many gaps in this overview.

Our easy walk downhill passed arched buildings like this Romeo and Juliet Renaissance balcony and delightful alleys. Carlo Moderno's 1746 fountain in the market place has 3 bees in a coat of arms. Pope Urban VIII's family were Barberinis = bees!

Everything demanded a closer look later in our day visit.

A well preserved Roman house has been excavated under today's modern street with mosaics, a bath and museum.

Examples of former layers of streets or buildings etc are always a little puzzling when they are uncovered like this.

It's worth remembering that Roman settlers had began the town 20 centuries ago before subsequent waves of occupation and abandonment led to disrepair and building over unwanted remains. Barbarossa had flattened Spoleto in 1155!

The spectacular Roman amphitheatre has the State Archeological Museum beside it with 3 floors of exhibits from the excavations, modern toilets, a lift etc.

It's not hard to see why Spoleto attracted EU funding as the theatre is an ideal setting for many festival performances. There's a second amphitheatre being restored lower down the town, Menotti's Teatro Nuovo, a contemporary art centre - hosting an international dance competiton which prevented us from looking inside, art galleries, various museums including textiles and costume and a modern shopping street, plenty to see and do.

It's a really exciting and interesting town with a city atmosphere: lots of theatre opportunities and enough shops to satisfy most people on a longer stay as well as being an excellent touring base.

It's worth considering Air B&B for budget travellers who shudder at the thought of camping. Friends have enjoyed stays round the world, often in self-contained apartments. That would have suited us when we had teenage children after outgrowing 'Le Bon Labourer' or Chambres d'Hote based in a farm (with pigs outside our door!).

One thing our group commented on was the lack of dedicated bread shops – because tourist trails include sales areas inside bars like these below, always beautifully presented and very tempting. We sat in the restaurant section of this popular businessmen's restaurant but only wanted a pastry. Usually the menu doesn't mention these so you choose and order from the bar display itself, at no extra cost. Always obliging, no one minds if you don't have a full meal.

Whatever the ticket price all Italian window displays are done beautifully, as this one for pasta and preserves.

Even behind glass it tempts us to buy produce we simply can't transport back to England in our small cases.

3 Assisi.

We had visited the famous birthplace of St Francis in 1985 in blazing August temperatures with our English Cosmos coach dropping us off right by the basilica for two hours en route from Rome to Venice. It was a different story on March 23, 2018 on the coldest imaginable day with truly biting inescapable winds gusting round every corner on the longish walk through the town from the excellent new car park. Assisi really stands out in the Vale of Spoleto, perched high on Mount Subasio above the main road north to Perugia stretched out like a sleeping dog, the head being the castle above the Basilica of the saint, similar to this view below.

Numerous churches with towers fill the hillside as we approach the main sights.

Born in 1181 into a wealthy cloth merchant family Francis had a privileged childhood, becoming an unruly partying teenager with dreams of becoming a knight. Held for ransom after being captured in a battle with Perugia he was imprisoned for nearly a year. Reputedly, he began to receive visions of God and heard His Voice telling him to abandon the life of luxury for one of poverty and to repair the Christian faith. Living as a peasant with no worldly goods he devoted himself to preaching in the countryside gathering followers and a growing reputation as a sociologist, treating everyone as equals even lepers who were normally outcasts. His love of people extended to animals and nature making him the patron saint of animals.

Franciscan monks, pilgrims and devout Roman Catholics are among the thousands of daily international visitors walking to the church complex erected to his memory. It holds a great art collection in beautiful buildings and is the 3rd most visited site in Italy. Giotto's paintings (from 1296) in the Upper Church reflect true-to-life faces, simple touches rather than their stylized Byzantine iconic precedents, a turning point, a rebirth of art telling stories about real people's lives. This *Renaissance*, this new way of thinking spread slowly but surely throughout Europe.

Our English guide took us from the modern car park up steps through the Porto Nuovo in the old town walls to St Clare's Basilica our first stop on our tour.

St Clare was his faithful follower who, like him, rejected family wealth to found her *Poor Clares*, initiating the monastic system of living in self-sufficient religious communities. Like him, she wore a simple cassock like the Franciscan pilgrim below, the habit of monks and nuns ever since. Theirs were displayed in her museum. Clare's white habit showed how tall she was. St Francis's brown cassock was much shorter.

Shops and cafes along the way were opening slowly to greet visitors. They wouldn't have much trade until after *the main event,* exploring the lower (1228-1230) and upper (1230-1253) churches and crypt (1818 – with his tomb) built by wonderful craftsmen to remember the Saint's life and work in 'repairing' the corruption within the Italian Roman Catholic church which put wealth and power above the kindness and humility which Jesus taught.

Her Basilica, supported by arches, is the first stop for all
guided tour groups like ours who lean against the wall on the
right to see the countryside of olive groves where St Francis
began his ministry below the steep slopes under the walls.

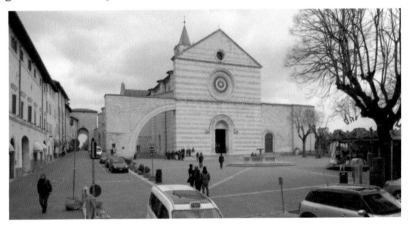

Tour guides minimise problems by explaining her story
before taking their turn inside without needing to speak
inside, a huge advantage with so many international visitors.

They explained St Clare's life and museum artefacts where groups could pay attention without being hurried. Otherwise imagine the disruption inside if the nuns by the entrance were Armenian and the group on the left had French teenagers. Unless you are connected by WIFI it's a struggle to hear your guide speaking anyway and just impossible if other guides are speaking loudly nearby in other languages. Ours was English! Relief all round!

It can be frustrating trying to decipher foreign pronunciation: even expected words are lost in translation. As a former English as a Foreign Language teacher I want to suggest hand-outs to see and hear key words simultaneously.

The extremely cold weather would drive most visitors inside eventually to eat, shop or look in galleries or museums waiting for their leaving time.

Summer crowds must be overwhelming but our visit was peaceful without any queues anywhere. We noted useful shops to return to later e.g. maps and local guide books.

There is no mistaking the famous white and rose coloured landmarks at the end of the Via St Francesco.

You approach the bottom church down the broad path beside the lawns after a routine safety bag check at the gates.

There's plenty of room for the thousands of daily summer visitors in the cloistered coutyard with wonderful views of the Vale of Spoleto below where Francis began his ministry of the value of poverty and simple faith. Groups can sit on the walls while waiting for their tour to go inside starting at the bottom.

We enter the hushed atmosphere of the lower church where frescoes and decoration resulted from nearly 100 years of work (after 1253) by different artists too numerous to identify here. What resonates is the turning point between portraying rigidly traditional figures in the story of the Passion and Life of Christ by adding little domestic touches like servants scaping left-overs into a dog bowl at The Last Supper (Rough Guide p 441).

Giotto's frescoes in the Upper Church (1296+) are the most famous. They include the saint's *Sermon to the Birds* and many historic biblical events. Thousands of visitors come just for the art treasures unlike ourselves who want to learn about all its history, even if we fail to absorb it fully at the time. Reading it up after holidays often helps to sort out what happened when how and why. It's often too much to absorb.

Wonderful pastry shops, art galleries, local craft and souvenir shops line the street back to the original Roman forum site in the Piazza del Comune's old buildings housing the tourist office, archaeological museum, cafes etc.

The Ç1 Temple of Minerva's Corinthian columns and pediment are excellent examples of a classical monument.

You can imagine the *'funny things'* that *'happened on the way to the Forum'* (Sondheim's famous musical) when looking around the square at the sheer variety of lovely buildings.

There would have been so much more to see up narrow steps or back alleys but we simply couldn't face exploring further in the biting winds and followed our guide into the ace Monnalisa Cafe Bistrot on Via Portica for fresh vegetable minestroni soup, a cheese and ham toastie, beer and hot chocolate (17 euros). It was a very enjoyable off-beat bargain in warm surrroundings.

We struggled to keep warm enough to enjoy the reat of our day in Assisi standing in patches of sunlight out of the wind.

4 Montefalco to Bevagna

Walking up the short, steep Via Umberto after leaving our bus outside this gate we are rather stunned by the mummified bodies in the Augustinian monastery (begun in 1275). Unlike their swathed Egyptian counterparts Beata Illuminata and Beata Chiarella's faces are seen through dusty muslin under glass. Truly old bones and yellow skin but sacred to Catholics.

No less than 8 saints were born in this very compact town resulting in some important art in the Ç14 Museo Civica di San Francesco and Pinacoteca and other churches. There was no spare time to see everything as we had a long cross-country downhill walk ahead of us.

We noted the famous 1522 Madonna and Child fresco, both with a halo and Jesus looking very wise and old as usual in these early paintings, always looking as if he is conversing with His mother.

Plenty of tourist shops and cafes were opening as we reached this beautiful medieval square, Piazza del Comune in the 'balcony of Umbria' with its all-round views.

It's reputed to be the best medieval square in Umbria, a lovely place to begin walking downhill to the cycle path to Bevagna. We totalled 22,000 steps that day (on my Fitbit watch), 14 km and really too much for most of us. The walk was scheduled as 10 km but felt more like 12.

Initially clutching at olive and fruit tree trunks in steep places, the path soon levelled off through vineyards on lower slopes.

There are 72 independent vineyards around here, renowned reds blended with the Sagrantino grape variety only found in Umbria. We certainly enjoyed both our local red and white hotel wines but the best Montefalco reds are world famous.

We saw blackened discarded vines contrasting with regiments of new vines, carefully wired to trail grapes along a low 'roof' for ease of hand picking for table use as seen in Puglia (kdp.amazon.com/vivien uff/Picture Walking Puglia) or mechanically harvested by ultra-sophisticated straddling tractors for wine processing (YouTube: Grape Harvesting).

Small bonfires were burning the prunings. It looked as undemanding as olive cultivation at this stage as a grower could manage single-handed but safeguarding young blossom and harvesting needs many skills and hands at precisely the right moment.

Cyclists passed us on the excellent traffic-free cycle path on the valley floor. Now there's a holiday idea for families!

The walls of Bevagna never seemed to get any closer. Borrowed sticks came in very useful. Heavy rucksacks became heavier as the sun forced us to shed some layers, a benefit which became a burden before we entered the nearest town gate in the Roman walls.

This first cafe was full and the town looked deserted so we were very happy to find a Tabac's side door open in Piazza Silvestri with a bench outside. The owner immediately sized up our needs, bringing a table outside to accomodate our beers, crisps and pastries to enjoy in brilliant sunshine. We really couldn't face sitting inside to have a hot lunch on a rare day like that. Trevor even shed some layers of clothing! Brill!

We could see the tourist office (officially the most unhelpful in Umbria, charging a euro for a free town map!) and toilet sign under the steps of the Ç12 Palazzo dei Consoli and admire the beauty of both the Romanesque churches opposite while saving our legs, content to let others tell us about the crypt in San Silvestro (1195) and beautifully carved gargoyles over the rose window of San Michele.

We were looking at the Corso Matteori, originally the Via Flaminia which had a staging post at Bevagna in 220 BC accounting for its renowned Roman remains. Our guide walked us to the Porta Cannara after pointing out a sea-creature Mosaic remaining from a bath complex and some tiny Roman houses with underground tunnels connected to the former amphitheatre stage.

It was warmer in Etruscan and Roman times as shown by thin clothing and exotic creatures in tomb frescoes and mosaics.

Bevagna's oldest streets were arched. Numerous sights were listed but most of us didn't have energy for exploring.

Annie enjoyed making us look at how far we had walked across the Vale of Spoleto from the distant Montefalco (falcon's nest) hills.

The Rough Guide suggests Bevagna as an alternative to Spello in the crowded tourist season - display board overpage.

Benvenuti a
BEVAGNA

Il centro storico
The town centre

PRINCIPALI MONUMENTI E PUNTI DI INTERESSE / Main monuments and places of interest

1. Porta Filippo Silvestri
2. Chiesa di San Francesco
3. Tempio di epoca romana
4. Mosaico delle Terme Romane
5. Porta Foggiole
6. Bottega medievale Gaita San Giovanni Cartiera
7. Ambulacro del Teatro Romano
8. Opera reticolata di epoca romana e cinta di mura medievale
9. Monumento ai Caduti
10. Ex Chiesa di San Vincenzo (antico quartiere ebraico)

11. Domus di epoca romana
12. Chiesa e Monastero benedettino di Santa Maria del Monte
13. Foro romano
14. Chiesa e Monastero agostiniano di Santa Margherita con Scala Santa
15. Chiesa di Santa Maria della Consolazione
16. Auditorium di Santa Maria Laurentia
17. Sede Comunale
18. Bottega medievale Gaita San Giorgio Zecchiere
19. Palazzo di Città (Museo, Biblioteca, Info Point)
20. Chiesa e Chiostro dei SS Domenico e Giacomo
21. Edificio portuale di epoca romana

22. Chiesa di San Michele Arcangelo
23. Palazzo dei Consoli ora Teatro Torti
24. Chiesa di San Silvestro
25. Chiesa di San Filippo
26. Bottega medievale Gaita San Pietro Cereria
27. Chiesa di Sant'Agostino
28. Epigrafi e basole romane Antica Via Flaminia
29. Bottega medievale Gaita Santa Maria Satificio
30. Cascata dell'Accolta sul Fiume Clitunno
31. Lavatoio pubblico
32. Porta Molini

PARKING

1. P.le Mazzi Micelli
2. P.le Trattati di Roma
3. P.le delM. Lugliesca
4. P.le Generale Sabbadi
5. P.le Giroria
6. Impianti sportivi

LEGENDA

- VIA ... PISTA CICLO-PEDONALE
- RISTORANTE
- HOTEL
- TOILET

MAPPA DEI QUARTIERI MEDIEVALI DELLE GAITE
Map of the medieval Gaite quarters

- GAITA SAN GIOVANNI
- GAITA SAN GIORGIO
- GAITA SAN PIETRO
- GAITA SANTA MARIA

Visita turistica delle Botteghe Medievali
Tourist visit of medieval workshops
www.ilmercatodellegaite.it

5 Lake Trasimeno

An unforgettable day seeing this huge Carp (12 KG?) caught
and then slid back into the murky water by this young
fisherman. Local bystanders were keen to tell me in gestures
and halting English that this was a common experience! But
my Cornish fishing background questions whether the huge
fish was actually a pet somehow kept in an invisible pen
ready to amaze tourists like those in Chinese legends and
Hungarian folklore. It was unfazed by having its cheek
stroked before being cradled back into the lake unlike
mackerel or pollock who thrash about to the death.

It was caught oposite our coffee stop, obligingly opened as soon as our guide telephoned the owner. The service, as always, was very efficient with every variation executed so willingly and without overcharging for this ideal location. We nearly got our order right with 'due Americano, molto, molto caldo latte' and didn't regret not ordering tea! Every cafe has at least one toilet, always clean if basic, with a reliable pull or push flushing system near the cistern once you find it!

We could see the ferries departing regularly from the nearby pier to the biggest island in the huge volcanic lake. Being Palm Sunday there were lots of visitors: 4 generation families - newest baby to great grandparents, groups like ours, young and older couples, uniformed scouts and guides heading to an island procession bearing olive branches and palm crosses to give away as they sang hymns walking ashore.

Passignano on the lake's north east shore is where Hannibal defeated the Romans in 217 BC, killing 16,000 men. The lake, never more than 7 metres deep in the volcanic crater, was the source of fish for Rome as explained in the small museum's paintings. Tree trunks were spiked into the 7 metre deep lake bed supporting nets holding caught fish. These nets were dragged off, full of live fish, and rowed to shore for horse and cart transporting to Rome together with animal produce.

Fish on Fridays wasn't just for Roman Catholics worldwide. It was observed in Cornwall until the 60's and elsewhere in England before becoming too expensive. We caught and dried our own before freezers arrived. Now its a trendy restaurant gimmick to increase trade, encouraging friends to socialise.

The little museum up some stairs on the main road (opened specially for our group) held other treasures: a wooden crucifix such as we had seen hung over many altars during our holiday and an early Madonna and Child altar group.

We had followed the ferry passengers up behind old houses on the main street up to the viewpoint and picnic area beside Ç12 Chiesa di San Michele Arcangelo with its enclosed cemetery and pheasants running around outside.

A guardian had opened the church to show visitors the old frescoes and current renovations.

These early frescoes are 2 not 3 dimensional in the Byzantine iconic style. What strikes us is that the repair cost must be huge for so few houses to bear (main street below).

After enjoying our picnic from a bench with views back to the mainland we walked past the dilapidated Villa Gugliemi (Villa Isabella to locals) which was built in the former 1328 Franciscan monastery. St Francis had lived on this island as a hermit from 1211. Now up for sale it had been an extravagant castle home from 1887 to 1975 for the Marquis Giacinto Gugliemi and his successors seen by them as dominating the island as in the paintings below..

The fishermen's houses depicted in the museum are now cafes with long outside seating areas extending to the waterfront but not used on a very cold day like ours. They would accommodate masses of visitors and pleasantly cool by the broad lake in summer.

Returning to our minibus on the 20 minute ferry trip back to Passignano the largely medieval houses hugged the cliffs and city walls behind the main road.

We strolled safely along the wide lakeside promenade at the end of a pleasant, if cold, visit. Picture it in summer? Fabulous

The camera does not lie! Spot the finger in the fish net cradle!

It took some encouraging but swam away slowly, unharmed. Our fish zoom off as soon as they reach sea water if they have to be put back because they are too small.

Is this Carp for real? Only Trasimeno residents know for sure.

6 Spello was our last and most interesting visit

It summed up the best of what we had seen in our 7 day **Ramblers' Adagio** holiday walkabouts in Umbria. And the sun shone all day to keep us happy.

You can see 30 interesting sights in the town but I shall focus on just a few. We walked from the bottom to the top, using the olive tree on top of a gate tower in Piazza Kennedy as a landmark and meeting place after by some Roman remains.

There is a free tourist bus in summer but it's easy and interesting to walk uphill getting to know what might be interesting to return to later e.g. the museum and art gallery, some arched and stepped alleys or a pleasant outdoor cafe.

We started with Santa Maria Maggiore's world famous Renaissance frescoes by Pinturicchio after an amusing guardian entertained us with his opinion of Prince Harry marrying a divorced commoner from Canada. He met us in the garden behind the church with some pruned olive stems left on the doorstep next door. It's an Italian Palm Sunday tradition hoping for peace and prosperity after the sadness of Good Friday and the joy of Easter Sunday.

His conservatory and nearby compact flower displays remind us that Spello has an imminent flower festival like Viterbo's. Italians achieve vibrant displays with small containers in very tiny spaces. The May/June *Infiorata festival* awards prizes for the prettiest lanes with terracotta tubs everywhere. Everyone collects petals to create flower pictures in streets. Spello's visitors match Lazio's for Viterbo's San Pellegrino celebrations (kdp.amazon.com/author/Vivien Uff/Picture Walking Around Viterbo. 2015) .

The side chapel of the often changed interior contains a ceramic pavement (1566) preserved under glass and 3 walls of Pinturicchio's (1454-1513) story-telling paintings describing the Annunciation, the Adoration of the Child and the Disputation in the Temple (Rough Guide pp 453-455).

An infamous Baglioni prelate had commissioned the chapel paintings in 1500 in typical one-upmanship style. Spello had 2,000 inhabitants and 100 churches in 1600!

The depth of Pinturicchio's perspective is very advanced.

Beyond the symbolism of various elements we can see how people lived in his Spello, their dress, farming, legends and the Umbrian countryside, true to life human stories with rounded characters typical of the Renaissance.

Back on the main street outside the plain exterior some wooden door panels are beautifully carved.

Further uphill restaurants are opening vast parasols on outside seating with a healthy breeze flowing past.

Opposite in our guides favourite modern boutique with tempting modern bags, jewellery and scarves, far removed from the usual tourist offerings.

A side street has a perfect Romeo and Juliet wooden balcony and street signs are worth photographing.

The art gallery and Roman remains in the open plan museum opposite could easily occupy an hour or so.

Advertisements for the flower festival (Infiorata) appear in side streets where open views remind us we are heading for the Roman aqueduct walking trail above the town.

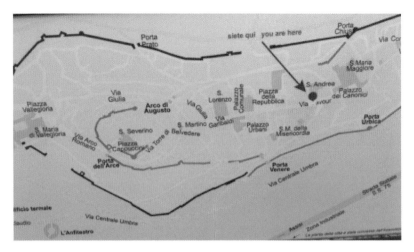

Some long-distance walkers pass us on the easy contour-hugging route while we relax by the cool fountain, watching a constant stream of people pulling up in cars or vans to refill lunch bottles and huge kitchen containers. Troughs match cattle, horses and dogs drinking heights: little and large, everyone can enjoy the pure, cold water.

We are back to where we started at Trevi in olive and vine countryside beside the aqueduct explanation.

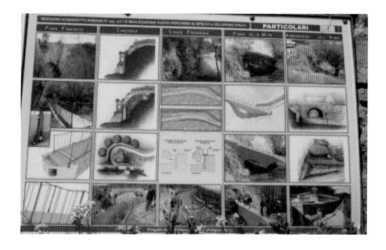

Broken sections nearby clearly show how the water flowed through a tunnel inside the aqueduct walls with wells for public collection sited at intervals along its length. Crops may have needed extra irrigation in warmer Roman times.

And home to our palatial hotel in the minibus after refreshment in a garden restaurant with fabulous views.

It's goodbye to our *Adagio Ramblers'* guided tour of Umbrian hilltop towns and back to our usual lives in the UK documenting this holiday while finishing our joint Japan account and reading up Catalonia, Sardinia and Corsica (next)

Author's note:

This is my 14th self-published Amazon digital 'walkabout', the 9th in my Picture Walking illustrated series helped by Trevor's photographs and geographical expertise. My native Cornwall round St Mawes and Falmouth, Yorkshire, France (2) and Italy (3) will soon be joined by Japan (1966 and 2017).

My 1st paperback Picture Walking Historic Almondbury sells locally and online. This Umbrian book will be my second.

Comments are welcome to ufftrevandviv@sky.com

Find me on Twitter @BVUff or @kdp.amazon.com/author/vivien uff.

I hope that our travels today might interest our grandchildren one day and that digital records will survive for posterity.

Printed in Great Britain
by Amazon

37342301R00043